MW00995863

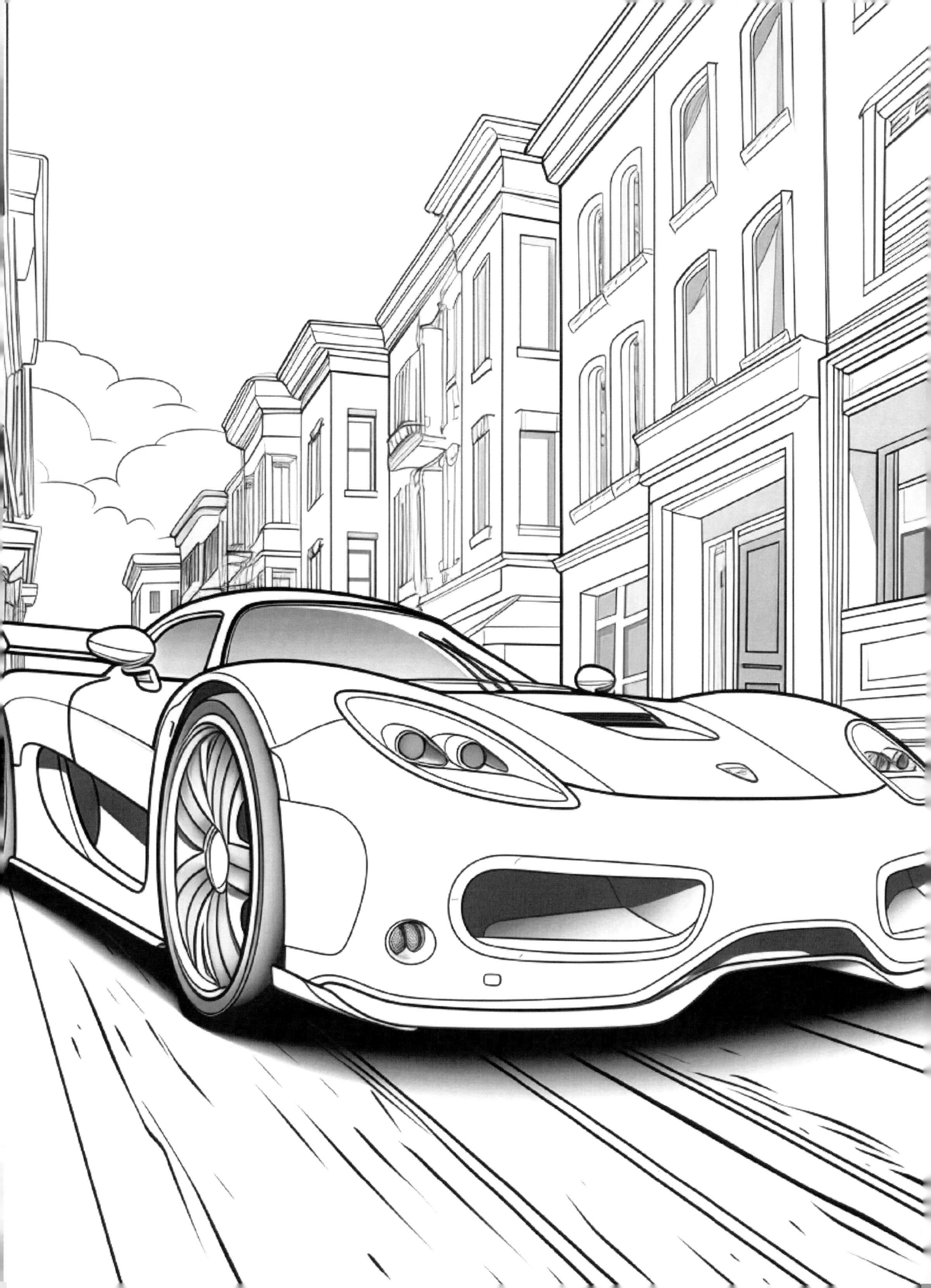

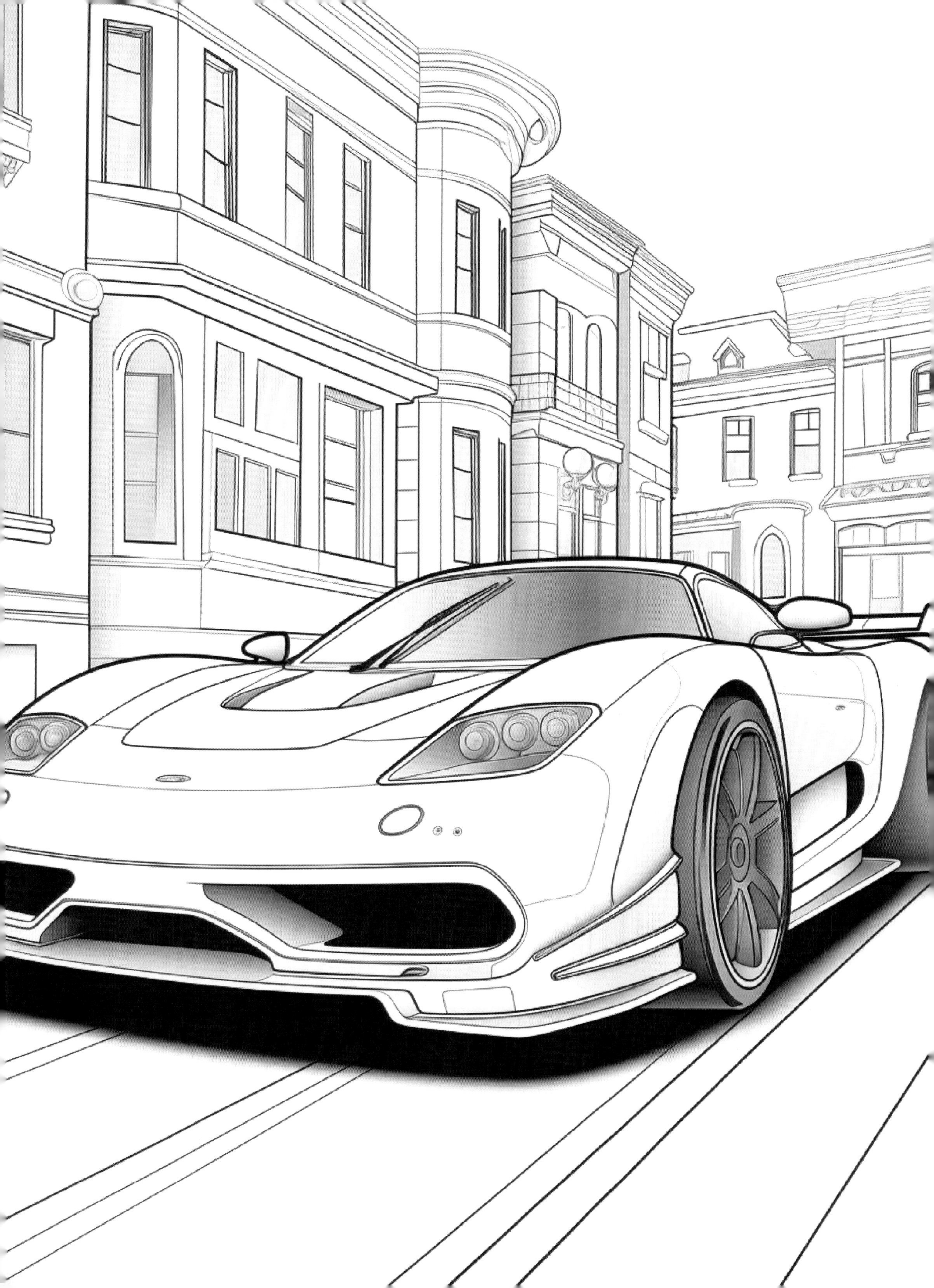

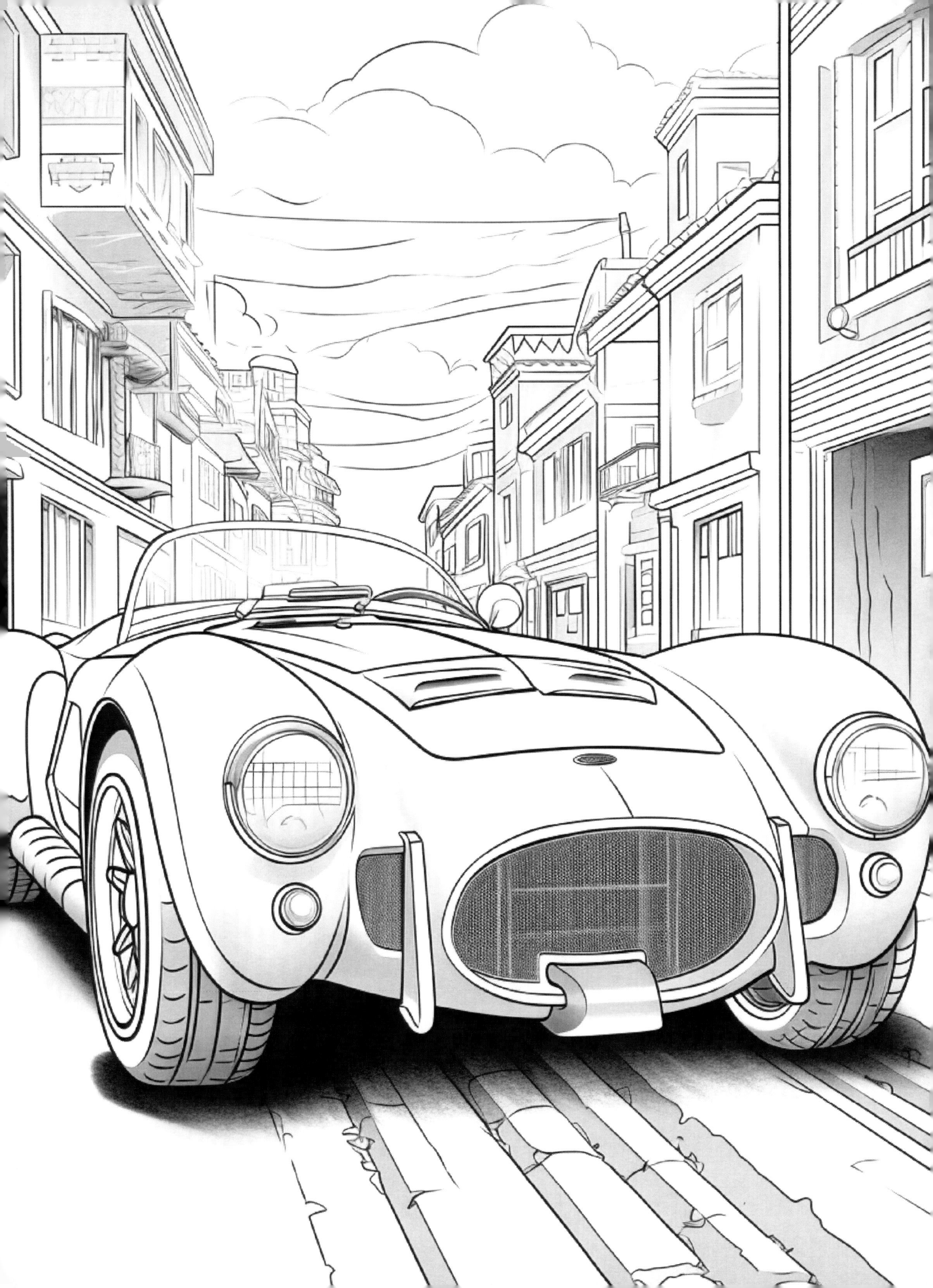

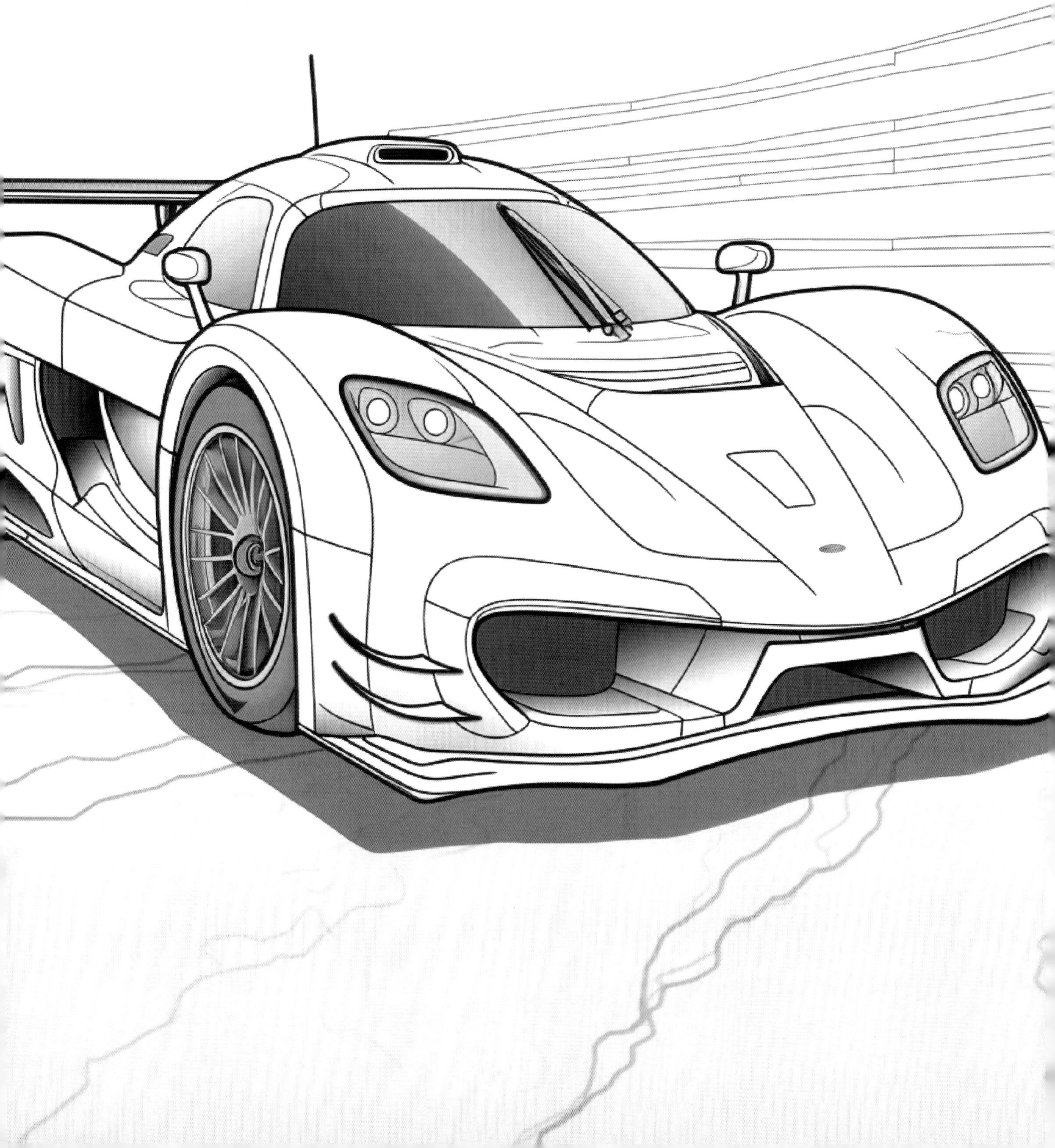

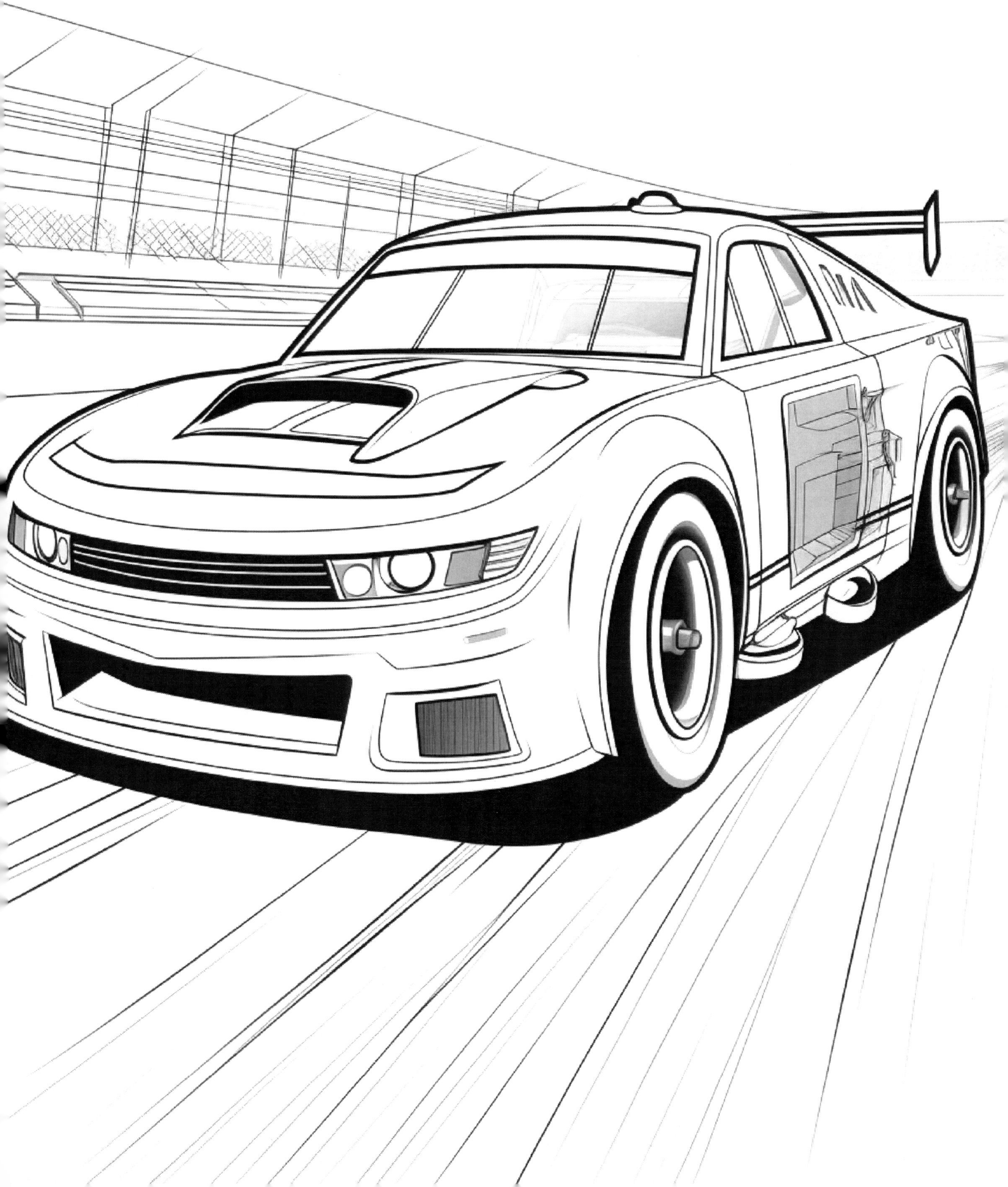

Made in United States
North Haven, CT
02 October 2023

42279801R00017